# BE RESILIENT!

## AN ACTIVITY BOOK FOR YOUNG PEOPLE WHO WANT TO SPRING BACK FROM CHALLENGES

**Kane Miller**

A DIVISION OF EDC PUBLISHING

First American Edition 2023
Kane Miller, A Division of EDC Publishing

© 2022 Studio Press
Text © Sharie Coombes 2022
Written by Dr. Sharie Coombes
Illustrated by Katie Abey
Edited by Ellie Rose and Frankie Jones
Designed by Rob Ward

First published in the UK in 2022 by
Studio Press, an imprint of Bonnier Books UK

For information contact:
Kane Miller, A Division of EDC Publishing
5402 S. 122nd E. Ave, Tulsa, OK 74146
www.kanemiller.com

Library of Congress Control Number: 2022934494

Printed in China
1 3 5 7 9 10 8 6 4 2

ISBN: 978-1-68464-536-7

# BE RESILIENT!

THIS BOOK BELONGS TO

_____

# WELCOME TO BE RESILIENT!

Author
**DR. SHARIE COOMBES**
Child and Family Psychotherapist

We all need a resilient spring in our step to help us cope with those moments that are big, new, scary, or difficult, or following unusual times. The spring means we can choose to keep going and take healthy risks to stretch ourselves, instead of giving up because we're worried about getting something wrong, making a mistake, or looking silly.

Doing these activities will help you understand what resilience is, how resilient you already are, and how to become even more resilient than you think you can be. You'll learn to recognize and manage your emotions and feelings when things are difficult, so you can keep trying and grow in confidence. You'll discover how to challenge yourself, be fearless in the face of adversity, bounce forward after a setback, and find out who can help you, ensuring that you enjoy your life to the fullest. Use this book by yourself or with a friend or an adult. Feel free to do a page a day or lots of pages all at once. Once you've completed the first few introductory pages, you can start anywhere in the book and come back to a page as many times as you want. You make the rules!

When worries feel enormous, you might believe nothing will help, but there is always a solution to every problem and nothing's so big that it can't be talked about and sorted out. You're not expected to BE RESILIENT! all by yourself – no one can be. Show some of these activities to important people in your life to help explain how you feel, if you want to. Talk to an adult you trust at school or ask an adult at home to take you to the doctor if you need more support.

Lots of us need a bit of extra help every now and then, and here are two organizations you can turn to if you're not comfortable talking to people you know. They've helped thousands of children with every kind of problem. They will know how to help you and will never be shocked or angry with you about what you tell them, however bad it feels to you.

## CRISIS TEXT LINE

Serves anyone, in any type of crisis, providing access to free, 24/7 support.

Connect with a trained crisis counselor to receive free, 24/7 crisis support via text message. Text HELLO to 741741

www.crisistextline.org

## NATIONAL SUICIDE PREVENTION LIFELINE

24/7, free and confidential support for people in distress. Call free or chat online. No matter what problems you're dealing with, whether or not you're thinking about suicide, if you need someone to lean on for emotional support or are worried about a friend or loved one, call the Lifeline.

www.suicidepreventionlifeline.org

1-800-273-8255

# THING-SPRINGS

## YOU CAN BE RESILIENT!

Since before you were born, you've been learning from all the THINGS that happen to you. Every THING counts, whether it's easy, hard, funny, upsetting, comfortable, challenging, joyful, scary, simple, frustrating — and all the other THINGS, too! These THINGS have already put the SPRING in your step and made you resilient.

Thanks to your experiences, you've grown invisible THING-SPRINGS. With the right care, your THING-SPRINGS will keep you bouncing forward and give you the confidence to tackle any big, new, scary, and difficult THINGS in the future. Without those THINGS to tackle, you'd never find out how amazing you are.

Let's meet your THING-SPRINGS, otherwise known as your resilience!

Everyone HAS resilience, including you!

Draw yourself on your THING-SPRINGS to remind yourself how resilient you are.

B-O-I-I-I-N-G

Everyone CAN GROW resilience, including you!

Resilience helps you cope with the tricky feelings that everyone gets. Just like every muscle in your body, the more you use your resilience, the stronger it grows, and the further it stretches. Having strong and stretchy THING-SPRINGS means you won't give up too easily or miss out on fun, excitement, and happiness.

Often, you learn most from the THINGS that go wrong or feel a bit too tricky at first. They supercharge your THING-SPRINGS!

List some THINGS you've experienced that have already helped to grow your THING-SPRINGS. They can be good THINGS or difficult THINGS.

I won a prize

My friend moved away

I helped my friend

My pet died

I didn't make the team

My teacher liked my work

BO-I-I-NG!

The activities in this book will help you take good care of your THING-SPRINGS so you can grow, strengthen and stretch your resilience, and build up your confidence. They'll encourage you to BE RESILIENT! and KEEP GOING, even when the going gets tough. So, let's get going. READY... SET... BOUNCE!

# THING-SPRING-O-METER

**HOW MUCH BOUNCE IS IN YOUR THING-SPRINGS?**

Show how resilient you already are on this THING-SPRING-O-METER.

Decide how far your THING-SPRINGS can stretch when you need to do something big, new, or a bit scary or difficult.

Color the THING-SPRING-O-METER to show how high they'd reach right now. This book will show you how to get them to stretch the rest of the way.

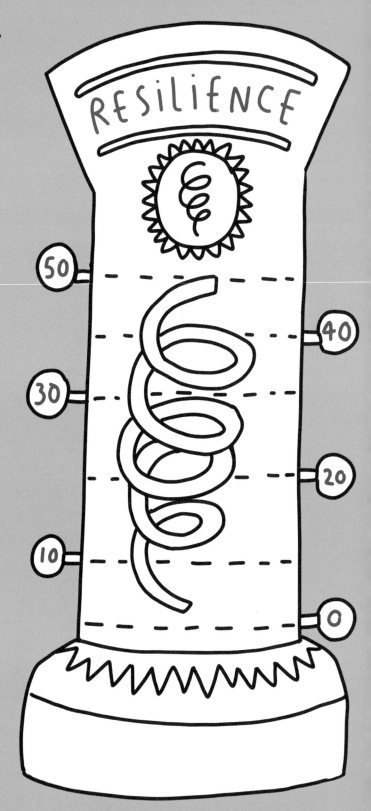

# THING-SPRING STRETCHER

It's time to strengthen and stretch your THING-SPRINGS.

Are you ready to collect some THING-SPRING points?

Whenever you complete an activity, color and collect the THING-SPRING points on the page, then add them to this THING-SPRING STRETCHER by coloring in the number of points you've earned – see how far you can go, and become a RESILIENCE SUPERSTAR!

For every THING-SPRING point you earn, color in one section. If an activity's worth three THING-SPRING points, color three sections, or if it's worth five THING-SPRING points, color five sections, and so on. If you repeat an activity, you can collect the points again!

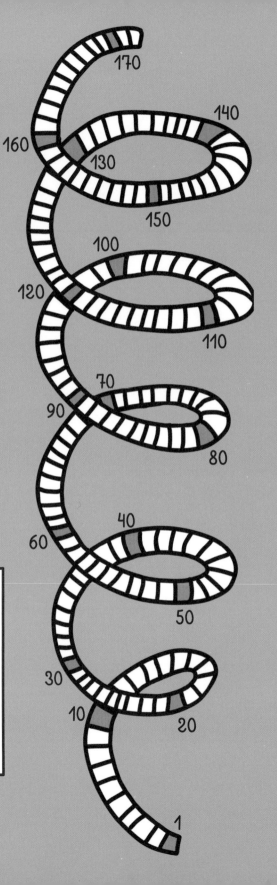

# YOUR HERO TEAM!

Your resilience can't grow super strong and stretchy all by itself. You'll need two teams around you to build the healthiest THING-SPRINGS!

The first is your inner HERO TEAM. Your HERO TEAM have their own superpowers and are all important parts of YOU!

## **H**OPE

Believes that good things are possible

## **E**NERGY

Puts effort into making good things happen

If you are neurodivergent and/or have ADHD, autism, or anxiety, it might sometimes feel harder to hear your HERO TEAM at first. Don't worry, you'll hear them more easily as you go through the book.

Design a colorful costume for each member of your HERO TEAM.
Think about their special qualities and try to work them into your designs.

You'll be seeing a lot more of your HERO TEAM
and getting to know all about them and their
jobs in the following pages. The activities will
train your whole HERO TEAM, so they'll be
ready to spring into action to support you
whenever your bounce feels a bit flat.

## OPTIMISM

Believes in the
power to succeed

## RESILIENCE

Believes in overcoming
challenges to KEEP GOING

THIS
ACTIVITY EARNS YOU
**FIVE THING-SPRING**
POINTS

# PICK YOUR OWN SUPPORT SQUAD

 You've got your HERO TEAM set up, so let's go ahead and pick your SUPPORT SQUAD.

 Everyone needs a SUPPORT SQUAD to grow healthy THING-SPRINGS.

**TOP TIP**  Pick your SUPPORT SQUAD members from your home, family, school, clubs, community, and organizations you belong to. Include people and pets and at least one of your favorite toys. Pick team members who are great at listening, encouraging, being funny, reassuring, challenging, cheering, or comforting you.

THIS ACTIVITY EARNS YOU FIVE THING-SPRING POINTS

Sometimes your resilience gets stretched as far as it can go for now, and that's when you need to ask an adult for help. It can take a little time for you to feel the spring in your step again, but it's still there and will bounce back with support.

Complete this set of SQUAD CARDS to remind you who can support
you as you grow your resilience. Draw their portraits and
add their important information to the cards.

NAME      RESILIENCE
POSITION      FRIEND
FAVORITE NUMBER      1
IS GREAT AT      HELPING
ME TO BE RESILIENT

NAME      _____
POSITION      _____
FAVORITE NUMBER      _____
IS GREAT AT
_____

NAME      _____
POSITION      _____
FAVORITE NUMBER      _____
IS GREAT AT
_____

NAME      _____
POSITION      _____
FAVORITE NUMBER      _____
IS GREAT AT
_____

NAME      _____
POSITION      _____
FAVORITE NUMBER      _____
IS GREAT AT
_____

NAME      _____
POSITION      _____
FAVORITE NUMBER      _____
IS GREAT AT
_____

Position means who
they are to you,
such as friend,
teacher, and so on.

Remember, you don't have to BE RESILIENT! by yourself, and
it's NOT all your responsibility. Use your SUPPORT SQUAD!

Now you can bounce
around all over this book.
Have fun – you've got this!

Remember to ask your SUPPORT SQUAD
for help to train the whole HERO TEAM,
whenever you need to.

# WHEN THE GOING GETS TOUGH

What happens to you when you do something that feels big, new, scary, or difficult? Perhaps you feel excited, anxious, stressed, nervous, scared, frustrated, or angry?

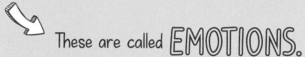

These are called EMOTIONS.

You might not always know the name of the emotion you're feeling, but it's important to learn to recognize the sensations you feel, and where in your body you feel them.

This is called INTEROCEPTION

(in-ter-o-sep-shun).

When you can identify your body's sensations, you can BE RESILIENT! The more you try to recognize your feelings, the easier it becomes to manage and confront them.

Think of a fun THING you'd like to do that's difficult to face or you're worried about. Write it in this box.

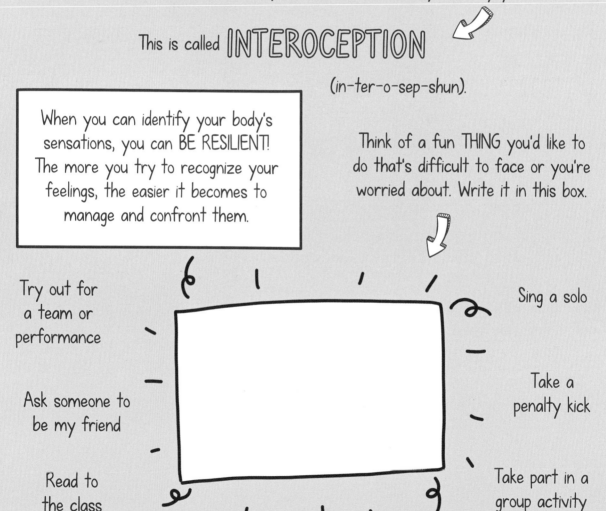

Try out for a team or performance

Ask someone to be my friend

Read to the class

Sing a solo

Take a penalty kick

Take part in a group activity

Draw yourself using the outline. Now, really imagine yourself confronting that THING. Circle any of the feelings you notice and draw an arrow to where you feel them.

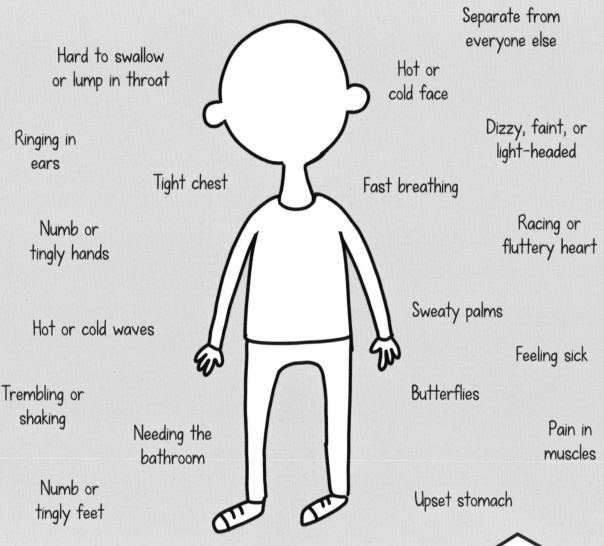

Separate from everyone else

Hard to swallow or lump in throat

Hot or cold face

Dizzy, faint, or light-headed

Ringing in ears

Tight chest

Fast breathing

Racing or fluttery heart

Numb or tingly hands

Hot or cold waves

Sweaty palms

Feeling sick

Butterflies

Trembling or shaking

Pain in muscles

Needing the bathroom

Numb or tingly feet

Upset stomach

The next time you have a challenge to face, come back to this page and go through the activity again to see what body sensations you notice. This will stretch your THING-SPRINGS and change how your brain copes with challenges – you'll soon be fearless! You can also come back any time you need to, to help you explain to someone what's happening for you.

THIS ACTIVITY EARNS YOU THREE THING-SPRING POINTS

# WHAT'S THAT YOU'RE FEELING?

Learning to BE RESILIENT! means coping with big, new, scary, and difficult feelings. You also need to be able to stay focused when you have good feelings and use them to help you achieve your dreams without becoming distracted.

Write or draw what THINGS make you feel these different emotions.

JOYFUL

CERTAIN

EXCITED

HAPPY

CALM

CONFIDENT

COMPETENT

CREATIVE

CAPABLE

It's helpful to recognize your feelings and accept that you'll have them because everyone has feelings. When you can BE RESILIENT!, you'll be able to KEEP GOING even when these feelings start climbing into your mind and body. When they start climbing in, welcome them and thank them for everything they can teach you about how to BE RESILIENT!

# HOPE SPRINGS

Every member of your HERO TEAM has an important job.

Meet **HOPE**. **HOPE** believes that good things are possible.

COLOR HOPE IN

Think about Hope's special qualities and update your earlier costume design for this picture. What good things do you believe are possible?

Write your hopes for yourself, others,
and the world on these sticky notes.

Keep coming back until you've filled all the
sticky notes, then add more if you like!

THIS
ACTIVITY EARNS YOU
THREE THING-SPRING
POINTS

# INFINITE GOOD THINGS

Every member of your
HERO TEAM
has an important job.

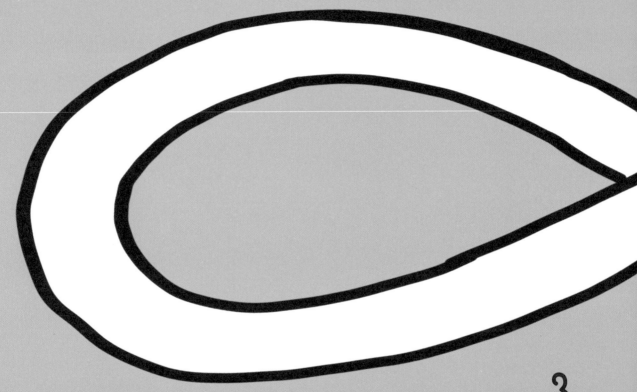

## 1
Trace your finger over the symbol, starting anywhere you like, and moving it smoothly to complete a sideways figure eight pattern.

## 2
Keep tracing and breathe in for one complete pattern until you get back to your starting point, then breathe out for the next full pattern.

## 3
KEEP GOING, following your finger with your eyes as it traces the symbol.

Why not tell someone from your SUPPORT SQUAD all about one of your hopes, if you'd like?

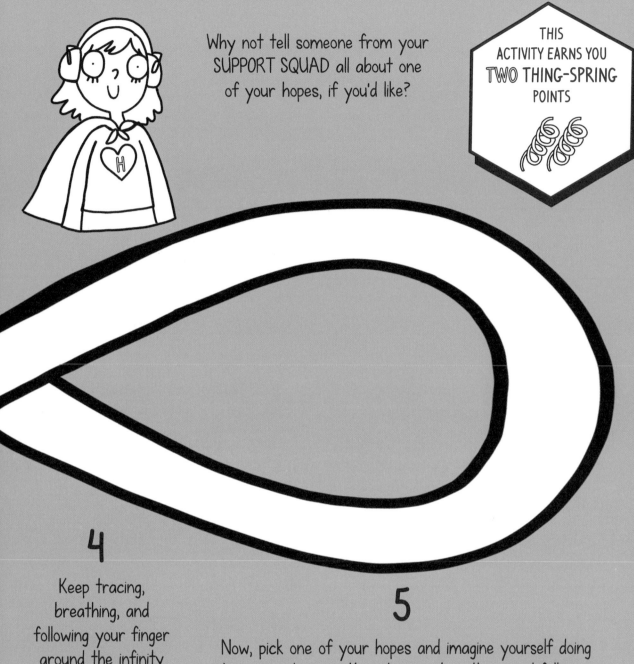

**4**

Keep tracing, breathing, and following your finger around the infinity symbol. Spend as long as you want doing this.

**5**

Now, pick one of your hopes and imagine yourself doing it in a mind movie. Keep tracing, breathing, and following your finger if you can, otherwise just concentrate on your breathing and mind movie. Go into a lot of detail and as you feel yourself achieving those amazing things, notice what you believe about yourself in that moment. Think about who is there watching you and what they'll be feeling. Spend as long as you want doing this.

# TO INFINITY AND BEYOND

You can do this activity anywhere outside that's safe. If you can't get outside, why not look out of a window?

Go outside, look up above you, and see what you can see. Look at the trees, tall buildings, airplanes, clouds, stars, birds, or at whatever is there.

Do this activity standing up, sitting down, or lying on the ground.

## SAFETY WARNING

Never look directly at the sun! Always make sure an adult knows where you are and that you are in a safe place.

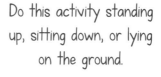

Now, imagine this infinity symbol is floating up in the sky and start to trace it with your eyes, making it as big as you possibly can. Breathe in for one complete pattern and out for the next, and then KEEP GOING like this.

If your symbol is huge, you might need to breathe in and breathe out once in each pattern. Spend as long as you want thinking about how relaxed you feel in this moment and how wonderful the sky is.

**TOP TIP** You can trace the symbol with your finger if it helps, but you can go bigger if you just imagine it.

KEEP GOING until you feel really calm and relaxed. Do this activity whenever you need to relax.

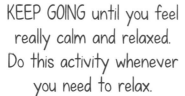
Your THING-SPRINGS need regular time off to rest, relax, and recover.

THIS ACTIVITY EARNS YOU **THREE THING-SPRING** POINTS

COLOR THIS IN

# I DESERVE GOOD THINGS

THIS ACTIVITY EARNS YOU TWO THING-SPRING POINTS

# NAME GAME

Your name is a very personal part of who you are. You and your SUPPORT SQUAD deserve some love, so let's give it!

Write your name in capital letters in this box, with the letters going down like this:

**H**OPE
**E**NERGY
**R**ESILIENCE
**O**PTIMISM

Write a word for each letter that describes your best qualities. Your words can begin with the letter from your name, or you can be really adventurous and include it within a word (you might need to put your capital letters near the middle of the box).

energy

Give your SUPPORT SQUAD members their own box and write their names in the same way as you did for yours. Add positive words about them using the letters of their names. Don't forget to show them what you think of them!

THIS ACTIVITY EARNS YOU **FOUR THING-SPRING** POINTS

# GO IT ALONE

Take yourself somewhere cozy, safe, and quiet within your home, without any devices or distractions. You could go into the backyard, if you have one.

Sit or lie down somewhere comfortable – take a pillow or blanket if you want.

Set a timer for 20 minutes and leave it where you'll be able to hear it. Or you could ask an adult to come and get you when the time's up.

Sit quietly with your own thoughts and focus on breathing calmly. Make your out-breath longer than your in-breath by breathing in for a count of three and out for a count of five.

Pay attention to what you can hear, smell, see, and touch. Notice what you feel on the inside of you. You could close your eyes if that feels nice. Treat all your thoughts like scenery passing you by from a moving car, bus, or train.

When the time's up, thank yourself for your excellent company!

## INTEROCEPTION

Always tell an adult where you are going and make sure it's OK with them.

THIS ACTIVITY EARNS YOU **TWO THING-SPRING** POINTS

# WHO ARE YOU?

Everything about you is special and you are so much more than what you can do.

Complete these sentences about yourself.

I'm loved by

..................................................................

I feel good when

..................................................................

I'm good at

..................................................................

I'm proud of myself for

..................................................................

I have great

..................................................................

THIS
ACTIVITY EARNS YOU
TWO THING-SPRING
POINTS

# WELL-BEING WALK

Spending time in nature is really good for your brain and body. It slows your heart rate, reduces stress and worries, and helps you to feel connected to something bigger than yourself.

Go for a walk in your local area with an adult or a friend for at least 20 minutes. Take this book with you to remind you what to do, or use a notebook to jot down the instructions. Ask for help from a member of your SUPPORT SQUAD if you need to.

**5...**

Listen to the sounds you hear. Try to pick out five different sounds. Don't think too much about what they are or where they are coming from. Focus more on how they sound to you and how you feel about the sounds. Some of the sounds might come from you as well. You are part of nature.

**4...**

Stand still or sit down and look at all the shapes, colors, and textures you see around you. Try to pick out four things that are pleasing to you to look at. Let your eyes drift over all the things you can see.

**3...**

Find three things you can touch. Be careful not to pick up anything dirty, sharp, or unsafe and don't pick anything that's growing – leave it for everyone else to enjoy. Maybe you can touch the bark on a tree or a soft blade of grass. Let your fingertips sense the texture of what they're touching.

**2...**

If you can stop somewhere safe, close your eyes and notice two things you can feel, such as the temperature of the air on your face, the crunch of the leaves under your feet, or the fabric of your clothes on your skin. Notice what they all feel like to you and which ones you like best.

Always tell an adult where you are going and make sure it's OK with them.

**1...**

Take a deep breath right where you are and find one thing you can smell. You might have to really concentrate to pick out a smell, but give it a try.

THIS ACTIVITY EARNS YOU TWELVE THING-SPRING POINTS

When you've completed the sensory part of this activity, just KEEP GOING and walk for as long as you like.

COLOR
THIS IN

THINGS CAN
ALWAYS
GET BETTER

# HERO STONES

What if you need a reminder that your HERO TEAM is right behind you all the time?

Make a set of supportive HERO stones that you can keep for just that kind of moment. HERO stones have encouraging messages on one side, and a HERO initial or logo on the other side. Hold them in your hands whenever you need help to BE RESILIENT!

You can enjoy their edges, lumps, bumps, and cool comfort as you hold them in your hands.

## INSTRUCTIONS:

1 Look in your yard, if you have one, for four smooth, flat stones, or choose from a small bag bought at a nursery.

2 Wash your stones in dishwashing liquid and warm water, then dry them completely on paper towel.

3 To decorate them, you can use stickers, cut-out pictures, acrylic paint, or permanent markers, as well as sequins, ribbons, gems, feathers, and other craft things. PVA glue works well for sticking things to your stones. You could also leave them natural.

4 Write your encouraging messages on each stone and keep them in your room at home to remind you whenever you need your HERO TEAM.

R

I HAVE THING-SPRINGS

GOOD THINGS ARE POSSIBLE

YES I CAN

I CAN AND I WILL

H

I CAN KEEP TRYING

THIS ACTIVITY EARNS YOU FOUR THING-SPRING POINTS

# AFFIRMATION NOTIFICATION

Affirmations are supportive words to say aloud to yourself to help you BE RESILIENT!

Take the hard work out of choosing an affirmation by getting an AFFIRMATION NOTIFICATION with these dice. Roll and recite whenever you need a bounce boost.

## YOU WILL NEED:

- Scissors
- Glue or sticky tape
- Colored pens or pencils

BE CAREFUL USING SCISSORS. ASK AN ADULT FOR HELP.

THIS ACTIVITY EARNS YOU **SIX** THING-SPRING POINTS

## INSTRUCTIONS:

- Detach the page opposite by cutting along the dotted line.

- Carefully cut out the shapes or ask someone from your SUPPORT SQUAD to help you.

- Add your own affirmations to the blank sides, then decorate each die as you wish.

- Assemble each die by folding along the dotted lines to make a cube, then stick together using the tabs.

- PLAY!

## HOW TO PLAY:

- Roll your AFFIRMATION NOTIFICATION dice and read aloud the affirmations they land on. If you have a mirror, look in it when you read the AFFIRMATION NOTIFICATIONS.

- You can play this game alone, with any member of your SUPPORT SQUAD, or absolutely anyone you want to invite.

- Why not make another set of these to give to a friend or someone in your SUPPORT SQUAD?

I AM NOT ALONE

I CAN DO HARD THINGS

I AM NOT MY MISTAKES

I AM NOT WHAT HAS HAPPENED TO ME

I HAVE STRONG THINGSPRINGS

I CAN TRY AGAIN

I CAN KEEP GOING

I AM GOOD ENOUGH

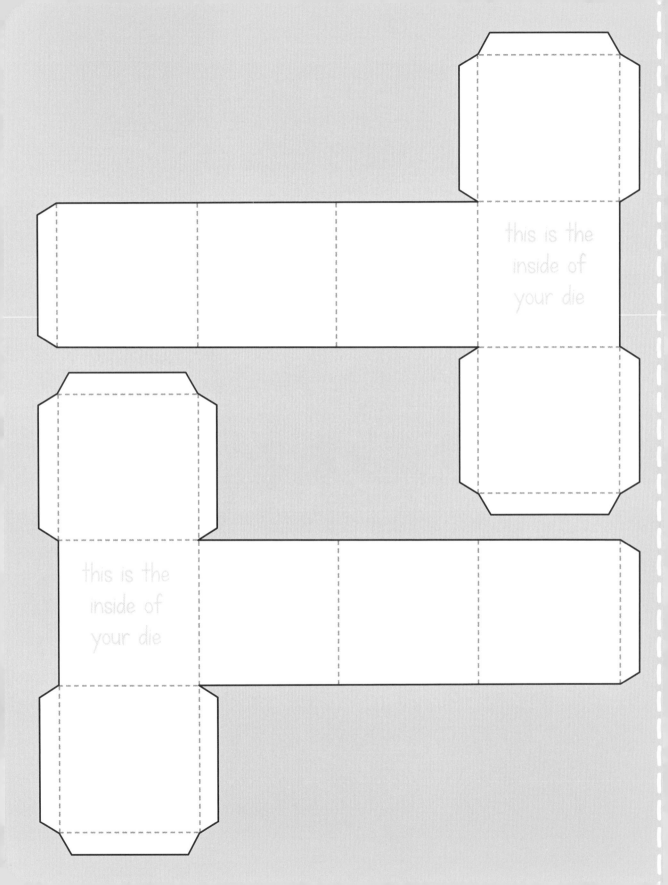

this is the
inside of
your die

this is the
inside of
your die

# TEAM TALK

Grab a cold glass of water and sit down with your SUPPORT SQUAD for a TEAM TALK.

If you can't get all of them together, that's fine – you can carry out this activity with them separately and have even more chances for fun.

## THERE ARE FOUR PARTS TO YOUR TEAM TALK:

1   Update the SUPPORT SQUAD on how things are going for you. Include anything big, new, scary, or difficult you've achieved.

2   Thank your SUPPORT SQUAD for their help – you could make a thank you card to give them at the TEAM TALK, if you want.

3   Tell each other the best jokes you know, while patting your head with one hand and rubbing your stomach with the other hand. Take turns and KEEP GOING for as long as you can.

4   If you'd like to, have a group hug with your SUPPORT SQUAD and plan when your next TEAM TALK will be.

THIS ACTIVITY EARNS YOU **THREE THING-SPRING** POINTS

# TAKE A BREATH

If you can stay in control of your breathing as you face a challenge, your energy goes where it's needed and you can feel confident. Noticing when your breathing gets faster or harder is an important skill that you can learn.

People who notice the changes in their breathing before their body and mind start to feel uncomfortable find it easier to BE RESILIENT! and KEEP GOING.

When you breathe out for longer than you breathe in, you feel safe, relaxed, and in control, so this 3:5 breathing skill is perfect for your THING-SPRINGS.

Sit comfortably and start to notice your breathing. Imagine you are breathing in courage and breathing out any worried feelings.

BREATHING COURAGE IN FOR 3...

... AND WORRY OUT FOR 5

After a few minutes, breathe in smoothly for a count of three, and then out slowly for a count of five.

As you breathe in, make the courage go all the way into your stomach. Put your hand on your stomach and watch it rise.

As you breathe out, gently push the air out from your stomach and watch your hand go back down as you let go of the worry.

KEEP GOING for a few minutes until you start to feel more courage spreading through your mind and body.

Enjoy feeling the courage spreading and KEEP GOING for as long as you continue enjoying it.

You can also use 3:5 breathing at bedtime to help you drop off quickly if your mind is busy.

THIS ACTIVITY EARNS YOU THREE THING-SPRING POINTS

# ENERGY BUZZ

COLOR
ENERGY IN

Every member of your HERO TEAM has an important job.

Meet ENERGY. ENERGY puts effort into making good things happen.

Think about Energy's special qualities and update your earlier costume design for this picture. What good things can you make happen by putting effort into them?

Write on these sticky notes what you want to put effort into in order to make good things happen for yourself, others, and the world.

Keep coming back until you've filled all the sticky notes, then add more if you like!

THIS ACTIVITY EARNS YOU
**THREE THING-SPRING**
POINTS

# I AM JAR

Turn a JAM JAR into an I AM JAR...

I AM GOOD AT SWIMMING

I AM HELPFUL

I AM SMART

## YOU WILL NEED:

- Your SUPPORT SQUAD
- A clean, dry jar with a lid
- Paper
- Pens
- Glue
- Stickers
- Magazine pictures
- Cut-out HERO initials or whatever you'd like to decorate the jar

Choose a really special pad of notepaper for this activity or maybe recycle some scrap paper into strips and keep them ready for action with the I AM JAR.

If there is a choice of jars, pick one with a shape you really like.

## INSTRUCTIONS:

- Make a label that says I AM JAR and stick it on the jar or the lid. Or both!

- Talk to the members of your SUPPORT SQUAD and ask them to tell you some things they admire about you.

- Together, turn each comment into an I AM statement.

- Write the I AM statement on a strip of paper, or type it up and print it out, then slip it into your I AM JAR.

- Write or type at least five more I AM statements of your own and tuck them into your I AM JAR.

- Keep your jar somewhere you can see it every day. If you're feeling wobbly, worried, or unsure, take out a few I AM statements and read them aloud to yourself three times. Doing this trains your HERO TEAM. It's a great idea to start every day by reading a few I AM statements.

What you hear about yourself is what you believe. What you believe about yourself is what you become.

THIS ACTIVITY EARNS YOU FOUR THING-SPRING POINTS

I AM CAPABLE

I AM PERSISTENT

# I CAN CAN

Let's celebrate all the things you CAN do!

You probably don't remember when or how you first did most of the hard THINGS you can do today. From now on, store everything you learn to do in this special can.

Also, whenever you are able to BE RESILIENT! and do something big, new, scary, or difficult for the first time, write it down and pop it in your I CAN CAN.

## YOU WILL NEED:

• An empty can with a lid

• Strips of paper

• Pens

• Glue

• Stickers

• Magazine pictures or whatever you'd like to decorate the can

You could use a clean and dry food can with some paper and a rubber band for the lid. Ask an adult to make sure there are no sharp edges and to put masking tape all around the top of the can for you.

## INSTRUCTIONS:

• Make a label that says I CAN CAN and stick it on the can.

• BE RESILIENT!

• Write down what you accomplished, then pop it in the can and put the lid on it.

• Shake the can as you shout out, "IT'S IN THE CAN!"

When you pop in a strip of paper, make sure you tell everyone how you were resilient.

Every now and then, go through your I CAN CAN and remind yourself how resilient you are.

THIS ACTIVITY EARNS YOU **FOUR THING-SPRING** POINTS

# BOB ALONG

Let me introduce
you to Bob!

Bob is the part of your brain that jumps in to
protect you from big, new, scary, or difficult things
and tells you not to try or that you can't do it.

Bob wants to stop you from taking any risks,
however small, which is useful when you're
crossing a road or using scissors, but not
so useful when you've got the chance to
go on a trip with your friends or you
need to do something for the first time.

COLOR
THIS IN

Bob responds really well to
a kind word, a gentle touch,
and the reward of seeing you
succeed. Show Bob how resilient
you can be and you'll train him
to let you take healthy risks.
As you color Bob in, tell him
some of the THINGS you'd
love to do and explain to him
why you think you could
do them, if he'd let you.

WRITE THESE THINGS HERE:

You could also tell a SUPPORT SQUAD member.

# DON'T GIVE UP!

We all fail. Every human fails, repeatedly. It's the ability to KEEP GOING that's the key to success.

Sometimes, what stops you from trying and succeeding with something big, new, scary, or difficult is the way it feels in your mind and body when you think about it.

You might worry you're going to fail, but failing is a supercharger and is nothing to be afraid of.

You might feel anxious, nervous, shy, or another unhelpful feeling.

It's normal to feel any of these THINGS, so accept whatever feelings come up for you and work around them rather than trying to stop them – remember, these challenges grow your THING-SPRINGS!

HELLO, BOB!

COLOR THIS SENTENCE IN AND KEEP SAYING THE WORDS TO YOURSELF WHILE YOU COLOR.

# I CAN ACCEPT THE FEELINGS AND KEEP GOING!

THIS ACTIVITY EARNS YOU TWO THING-SPRING POINTS

# MENTAL HEALTH

Everyone has mental health, just like everyone has physical health. Sometimes it's all going well and other times it needs a bit of help. There are some THINGS you need to have in your life in order to stay as healthy as possible, both mentally and physically.

Color in the check marks for all the things you already have in your life and circle anything on the list you don't have enough of.

Talk to a SUPPORT SQUAD member to make a plan to get more of what you need in your life.

FOOD ✓    SAFETY ✓

WATER ✓    FUN ✓

WARMTH ✓    LOVE ✓

AFFECTION ✓

CHOICES ✓

BELONGING ✓

SUPPORT ✓

CHALLENGES ✓

PRIVACY ✓

THIS ACTIVITY EARNS YOU **TWO THING-SPRING POINTS**

PLAN

# LETTERS THANK

Thanking people makes them feel good and boosts the bounce in their THING-SPRINGS.

WRITE A LETTER TO SAY THANK YOU TO SOMEONE BELOW.

You could remind them what they did and explain the difference it made to how you feel about yourself, what it meant to you, and how it helped you. You could also say how you will manage things in the future.

Why not write the letter out on paper and send it to the person you wish to thank?

EARN FOUR THING-SPRING POINTS IF YOU WRITE OUT AND SEND YOUR LETTER TO THE PERSON.

THIS ACTIVITY EARNS YOU **TWO THING-SPRING** POINTS

# BOTTLED UP

Sometimes, we bottle up unhelpful THINGS, and let them fizz away inside our minds, weakening our THING-SPRINGS. We often forget the helpful THINGS and let them evaporate instead of letting them make our THING-SPRINGS stronger.

In this bottle are THINGS that others have said to you, or about you, that have made you feel LESS confident. It's time for you to unbottle those words and let them go.

Write or draw these unhelpful THINGS in the bottle.

THIS
ACTIVITY EARNS YOU
TWO THING-SPRING
POINTS

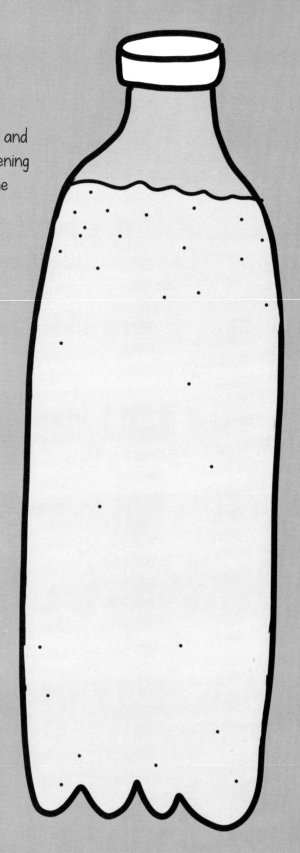

# YOGA

Yoga is an amazing way to grow strong and stretchy THING-SPRINGS. Everyone can do yoga – it's okay to change the movements so that they work for you and your unique body.

## WARRIOR 1 POSE:

- Sit or stand up straight, with your feet together and your arms out to your sides.

- If you're standing, step forward on one leg, bending your front knee, but keeping your back leg straight behind you. Otherwise, bend your knees.

- Arch your back slightly and stretch your arms and hands up to the sky.

- Look straight ahead with a strong expression on your face.

- Take a deep breath in for a count of three.

- As you breathe out, say aloud, "I AM STRONG."

- Stay in the pose and do this three more times.

- Breathing normally, bring your arms down to your sides and your feet back together. Sit with knees bent, or stand up straight.

- Switch legs and repeat.

I AM STRONG.

## HERO POSE:

- Smile and sit with knees bent, or kneel down, sitting gently on your heels. Rest your hands on your lap. Breathe calmly for a little while.

- Finish by repeating aloud three times, "I AM A HERO."

I AM A HERO.

## WARRIOR 2 POSE:

- Repeat the steps for Warrior I pose with your arms out to your sides.
- Turn your torso and stretch one arm out in front of you and the other behind you.
- Look straight ahead with a confident expression on your face.
- Take a deep breath in for a count of three.
- As you breathe out, say aloud, "I CAN DO HARD THINGS."

- Stay in the pose and do this three more times.
- Breathing normally, bring your arms down to your sides and your feet back together. Stand or sit up straight.
- Switch legs and repeat.

I CAN DO HARD THINGS.

## WARRIOR 3 POSE:

- Repeat the steps for Warrior I, but bring both arms up in front of you.
- Sit and lift your feet off the ground a little, or stand and straighten your front leg slightly, keeping your knee soft, and lift your back foot off the ground a little.
- Open your arms wider for balance, if you need to.
- Look straight ahead with a relaxed expression on your face.
- Take a deep breath in for a count of three.
- As you breathe out, say aloud, "I CAN BE RESILIENT!"

- Stay in the pose and do this three more times.
- Breathing normally, bring your arms down to your sides and your feet back together. Sit with your feet on the floor, or stand with your feet back together and legs straight.
- Switch legs and repeat.

I CAN BE RESILIENT!

# BOOST YOUR BOUNCE

Feeling flat? Give yourself a bounce boost and improve your strength, stretch, and balance.

Let's get your THING-SPRINGS moving. You can increase how many you do of each activity, adding a few more every time.

## STAR JUMPS

Sit or stand up straight with your feet together and your arms by your sides. Jump, moving your feet apart as you bring your arms out and above your head. Then immediately jump them back to your start position. Start with 10 of these and build up to more as you feel your fitness improving.

## ARM CIRCLES

Sit or stand up straight with your arms stretched out on either side of your body. Slowly move your arms in circles. This is to warm up your arms for the balance skills.

## BALANCE BOUNCES

Sit or stand up straight on one leg and tuck the other one behind you off of the floor. Stretch your arms out to your sides for balance, then bend your standing knee and gently bounce. Build up the bounce gradually so you keep your balance. Do this for as long as you can, then switch to the other leg and repeat.

## BALANCE STRETCHES

Sit or stand up straight on one leg and bend the other leg up in front of you. Stretch your arms out to the sides for balance, then stretch your bent leg out in front of you and hold it in place. Move your leg to the side and hold it in place, then move it behind you and hold it before returning your foot to the ground. Repeat this sequence five times, then switch to the other leg and repeat five times.

When you feel that your balance has improved, try the Balance Bounces and Balance Stretches with your arms by your sides.

THIS ACTIVITY EARNS YOU FIFTEEN THING-SPRING POINTS

# ONE SMALL STEP

If you want to make a giant leap, you'll have to take a lot of small steps!

What do you want to get better at or try for the first time? It can be something little, something you have to do, or something amazing you want to achieve.

Whatever it is will be a giant leap when you've achieved it.

WRITE WHAT YOUR GIANT LEAP IS IN THIS PLANET.

WRITE IN THIS STAR WHAT YOU'LL BELIEVE ABOUT YOURSELF WHEN YOU MAKE IT.

Complete the picture however you like and fill out these footprints to help you work out how you're going to make your giant leap. You don't have to use all the footprints, or you can add more if you need to. Ask a member of your SUPPORT SQUAD if you need help breaking your giant leap down into smaller steps.

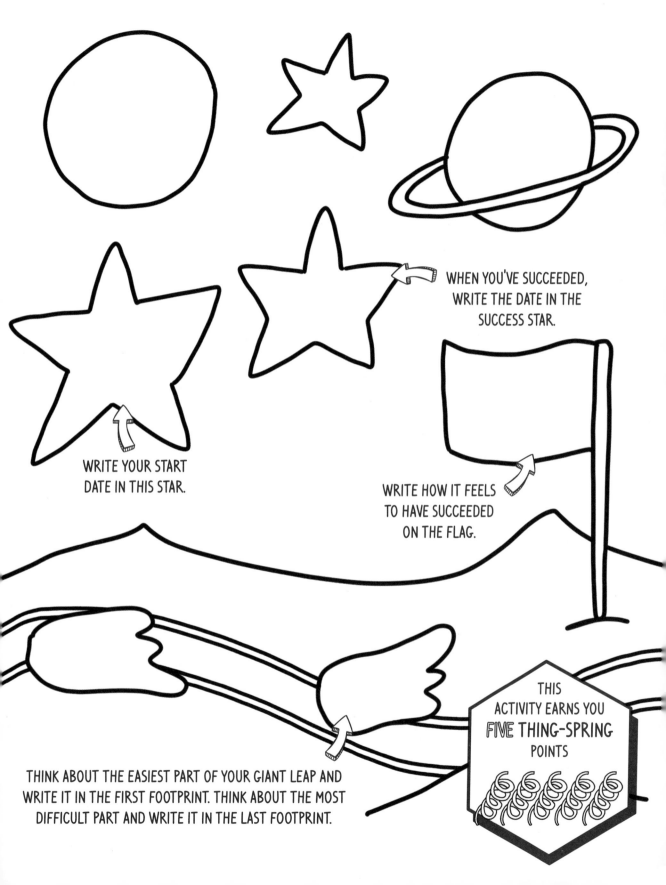

WHEN YOU'VE SUCCEEDED, WRITE THE DATE IN THE SUCCESS STAR.

WRITE YOUR START DATE IN THIS STAR.

WRITE HOW IT FEELS TO HAVE SUCCEEDED ON THE FLAG.

THIS ACTIVITY EARNS YOU FIVE THING-SPRING POINTS

THINK ABOUT THE EASIEST PART OF YOUR GIANT LEAP AND WRITE IT IN THE FIRST FOOTPRINT. THINK ABOUT THE MOST DIFFICULT PART AND WRITE IT IN THE LAST FOOTPRINT.

# DANCEARAMA

Dancing is a great way to stretch your THING-SPRINGS and feel fully free. Grab a friend, play some music, and dance like you are trying to reach the stars.

Invite your SUPPORT SQUAD, if you like. Not everyone loves to dance in front of other people, so feel free to get moving on your own if you prefer.

Dancing helps you feel better and moving helps our minds recover from big, new, scary, and difficult THINGS more quickly.

THIS ACTIVITY EARNS YOU TWO THING-SPRING POINTS

Go on! Sing along at the top of your voice and bounce your body every which way you can.

# MANDALA MAGIC

Color these mandalas using colors that make you feel good.

As you color them, notice how the mandalas are made from layers of pattern, starting with a strong center and getting more adventurous as they grow.

# RESILIENCE STRETCHES

Every member of your HERO TEAM has an important job.

Meet RESILIENCE. RESILIENCE believes in overcoming challenges to KEEP GOING.

COLOR RESILIENCE IN

Think about Resilience's special qualities and update your earlier costume design for this picture. What challenges can you overcome when you KEEP GOING?

Write on these sticky notes the challenges you're going to overcome for yourself, others, and the world when you KEEP GOING.

Keep coming back until you've filled all the sticky notes, then add more if you like!

THIS ACTIVITY EARNS YOU **THREE THING-SPRING** POINTS

# STREEEEEEEETCH YOUR THING-SPRINGS

When you want to BE RESILIENT!, do you need to be reminded how bouncy and stretchy your THING-SPRINGS are? Perhaps you worry you can't do something, but you wish you could? Let's train the whole HERO TEAM.

Cut out and hang up these THING-SPRINGS somewhere you will be able to watch them bounce, then sit back and remember how stretchy your own invisible THING-SPRINGS are.

## INSTRUCTIONS:

• Write all of the things you've gotten better at, tried for the first time, tried again, or overcome in the past on the first THING-SPRING.

• Write anything big, new, scary, or difficult you'd like to get better at, try for the first time, try again, or overcome on the second THING-SPRING.

• Cut out the whole page along the dotted line, then cut out the big circles that are going to be your THING-SPRINGS.

• Decorate your THING-SPRINGS however you want.

• Carefully cut around the dotted lines to create your THING-SPRINGS.

• Use yarn, ribbon, string, or elastic to hang up your THING-SPRINGS and enjoy watching them bounce.

THIS ACTIVITY EARNS YOU **THREE THING-SPRING** POINTS

# YOUR KIND OF FRIEND

Want to help someone else grow strong and stretchy THING-SPRINGS? Life's more fun when others can bounce confidently with you.

Write some helpful comments you would say to a friend who is finding something difficult or who worries about not being able to do something well enough. Be as supportive and encouraging as you can to help them BE RESILIENT!

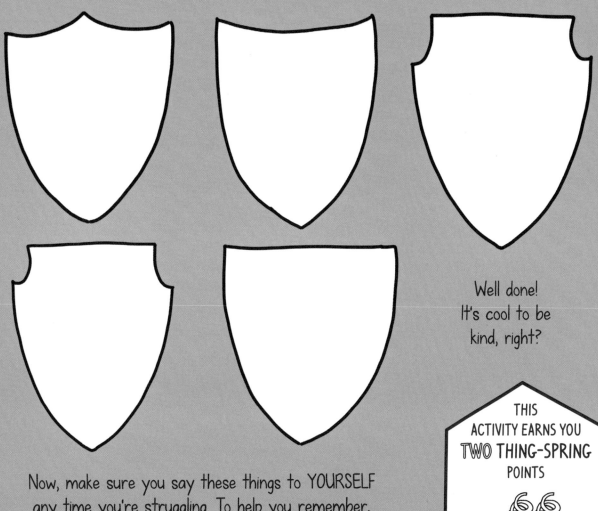

Well done! It's cool to be kind, right?

Now, make sure you say these things to YOURSELF any time you're struggling. To help you remember, why not write these out on sticky notes or pieces of paper and stick them to a mirror or above your bed?

THIS ACTIVITY EARNS YOU **TWO THING-SPRING** POINTS

# BOUNCE-ABILITY

Not every day is the same. As you grow your THING-SPRINGS, some days you'll feel more resilient, but on others it will feel so much harder to BE RESILIENT! The more often you try, the easier it gets. Use these pages to keep a diary of how resilient you feel and how much bounce you have in your THING-SPRINGS.

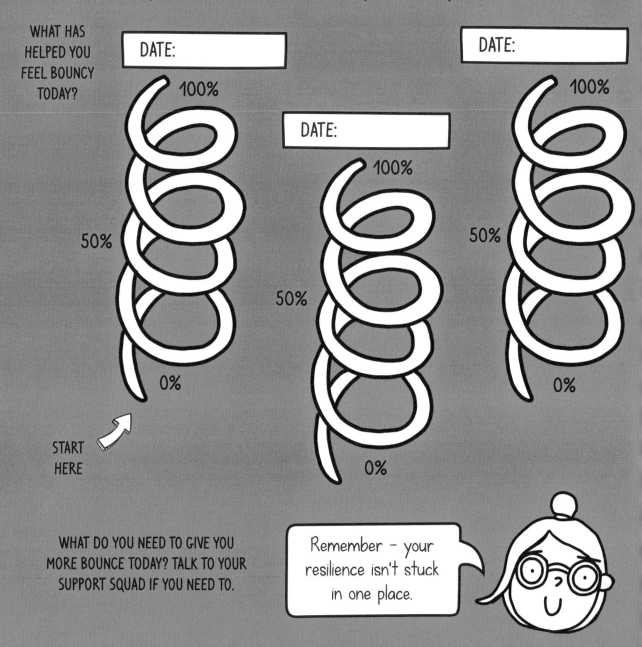

WHAT HAS HELPED YOU FEEL BOUNCY TODAY?

DATE:

100%

50%

0%

START HERE

DATE:

100%

50%

0%

DATE:

100%

50%

0%

WHAT DO YOU NEED TO GIVE YOU MORE BOUNCE TODAY? TALK TO YOUR SUPPORT SQUAD IF YOU NEED TO.

Remember – your resilience isn't stuck in one place.

Try to come back to these pages every day for a week so you can see how every day is different. If you forget, don't worry, just come back when you remember until all the THING-SPRINGS are sprung!

DATE:

100%

50%

0%

DATE:

100%

50%

0%

DATE:

100%

50%

0%

DATE:

100%

50%

0%

Color your springs to show how bouncy your THING-SPRINGS are today. If you get to the top on some days, write what helped you feel so bouncy.

THIS ACTIVITY EARNS YOU **TWO THING-SPRING** POINTS

# SPOT THE DIFFERENCE

Get your HERO TEAM working for you.

Try to spot the difference in your thoughts and beliefs when you train your own HERO TEAM.

| | | |
|---|---|---|
| I won't be any good at dancing.  | HOPE believes that good things are possible. | I might be surprised at how good my dancing is. |
| Riding a bike is too hard for me.  | ENERGY puts effort into making good things happen. | I can break it down into smaller steps and try hard. |
| I can't count backward.  | RESILIENCE believes in overcoming challenges to KEEP GOING. | I can't do it yet, but I'll ask for help and keep trying. |
| I'll never make the team.  | OPTIMISM believes in the power to succeed. | I might make the team, but if I don't, I'll be proud I tried. |

Using your HERO TEAM to spot the difference like this is called REFRAMING your thoughts and beliefs.

REFRAME SOME OF YOUR OWN THOUGHTS AND BELIEFS BELOW.

| | | |
|---|---|---|
| ................................ ................................ | HOPE believes that good things are possible. | ................................ ................................ |
| ................................ ................................ | ENERGY puts effort into making good things happen. | ................................ ................................ |
| ................................ ................................ | RESILIENCE believes in overcoming challenges to KEEP GOING. | ................................ ................................ |
| ................................ ................................ | OPTIMISM believes in the power to succeed. | ................................ ................................ |

# HERO PACK

Every HERO needs a HERO PACK full of THINGS they love. Make yours and fill it with the THINGS you love to see, touch, smell, taste, or listen to. Have it ready for those days when your bounce doesn't feel very strong and stretchy. The contents of your box should make you feel super bouncy in an instant.

## YOU WILL NEED:

• A shoebox or something similar (an old lunchbox or ice cream tub will work well)

Decorate the box however you wish with paint, wrapping paper, old comics, fabric, ribbons, posters, cut-out pictures – anything that expresses who you are.

## HERE ARE SOME IDEAS FOR WHAT TO INCLUDE:

- soft toys
  - music
- modeling clay
  - cloth
- hand lotion
- stress ball
- fidget toys
- pom-poms

- friendship bracelets
- rubber bands
- Bubble Wrap
- HERO stones
  - beads
- old tickets
  - bubbles
  - slime

- piece of fabric sprayed with your favorite scent
- your favorite collector card or toy
  - this book
- puzzle book
- small mirror

- bubble bath
- old birthday cards from special people
- your I AM JAR
- your I CAN CAN

THIS ACTIVITY EARNS YOU NINE THING-SPRING POINTS

Why not make a HERO PACK for a friend or a member of your SUPPORT SQUAD to help them BE RESILIENT! too?

# OPTIMISM WINS

Every member of your HERO TEAM has an important job.

Meet **OPTIMISM**. **OPTIMISM** believes in the power to succeed.

COLOR OPTIMISM IN

Think about Optimism's special qualities and update your earlier costume design for this picture. What do you believe you can succeed at?

Write on these sticky notes what you believe you can succeed at for yourself, others, and the world.

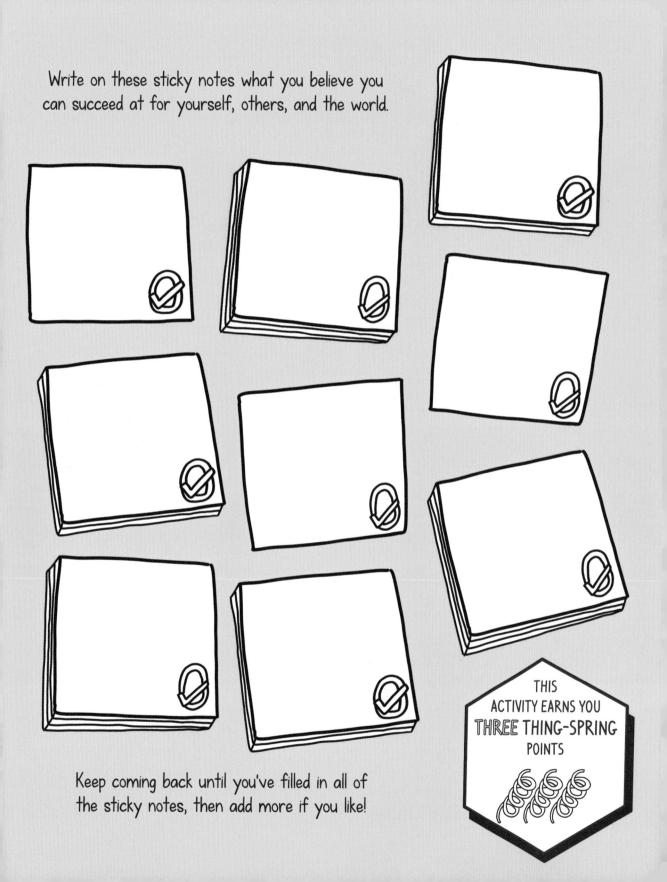

Keep coming back until you've filled in all of the sticky notes, then add more if you like!

THIS
ACTIVITY EARNS YOU
THREE THING-SPRING
POINTS

# FALL DOWN 7 TIMES, STAND UP 8

An old Japanese proverb says "Nana korobi, ya oki."

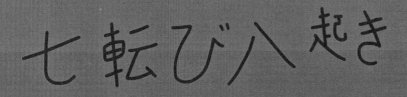

However many times you fall or fail, you must try one more time until you succeed. It won't always be as many as eight times that you have to try, but sometimes it might be more!

"Fall down seven times, stand up eight."

**PICK ONE GOAL YOU'D LIKE TO ACHIEVE. WRITE IT IN THIS BOX.**

You have to imagine you'll succeed and then KEEP GOING to make it happen. That's what it takes to BE RESILIENT!

Write or draw what happens in one of the boxes each time you try. KEEP GOING until you achieve your goal. If you need more boxes, add them on a piece of paper.

Do this for as many goals as you want – just make your own boxes on a piece of paper and go for it!

THIS ACTIVITY EARNS YOU **EIGHT** THING-SPRING POINTS

# A DIFFERENT WAY

It's important to KEEP GOING when you're trying to achieve something big, new, scary, or difficult.

Sometimes the best way to KEEP GOING is to change direction after a rest, and come at the problem in a different way or from a different direction.

Write the THING you want to achieve on the sign in the middle of the puzzle. Follow the lines to unravel which way works best to get to your goal. KEEP GOING and try all the different ways until you get there!

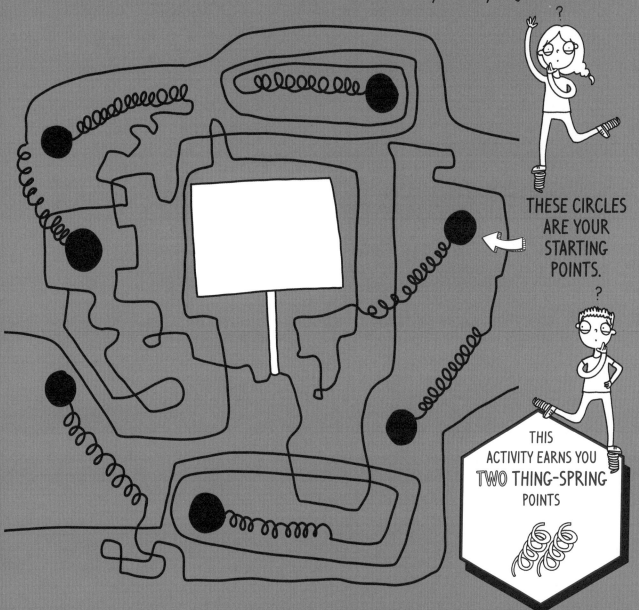

THESE CIRCLES ARE YOUR STARTING POINTS.

THIS ACTIVITY EARNS YOU **TWO THING-SPRING** POINTS

# WEIGHT OF THE WORLD

Some big, new, scary, or difficult THINGS feel so heavy and bring us down, making us forget we have any bounce in our THING-SPRINGS.

Write on the weights the THINGS that bring you down and make you lose your bounce. Talk them through with a SUPPORT SQUAD member if you want.

Does this ever happen to you? Me too! I like to imagine myself cutting the strings on these THINGS, one by one, to release my THING-SPRINGS from the weight of them and recover my bounce. Why don't you give it a try? SNIP, SNIP, SNIP!

THIS ACTIVITY EARNS YOU **TWO THING-SPRING** POINTS

When you've cut your THING-SPRING STRINGS, try saying, "I'VE SNIPPED MY THING-SPRING STRINGS" out loud 10 times and see what happens!

# HEARTY THANKS

Fill these hearts with all the things that fill your heart with gratitude. Include all the people, places, pets, or anything else you love and feel thankful for.

These THINGS lift you up high on your THING-SPRINGS when you feel weighed down. They help you feel bouncy!

THIS ACTIVITY EARNS YOU TWO THING-SPRING POINTS

# MIND MONSTERS

When you let yourself think you can't do something big, new, scary, or difficult, then you find horrid doubts about yourself creeping into your mind.

These doubts are your MIND MONSTERS and they LOVE to win! They destroy the good things you believe about yourself and can quickly make you feel unhappy, anxious, and worried because of what they tell you.

You're not good enough!

CONFIDENCE

YES, I AM GOOD ENOUGH!

They'll think you're silly!

PRIDE

They'll be mean to you!

HAPPINESS

The worst way to deal with your **MIND MONSTERS** is to agree with them, as this gives them all the power and they get stronger. The best way to deal with them is to use your own power and show them kindness, patience, and encouragement.

You'll become fearless in the face of these **MIND MONSTERS** if you work with Optimism.

I BELIEVE IN MY OWN POWER TO SUCCEED!

They won't like you!

SELF-ESTEEM

You're going to fail!

COURAGE

Write in the boxes what you think Optimism would say to these **MIND MONSTERS**.

THIS ACTIVITY EARNS YOU **TEN THING-SPRING** POINTS

# LETTERS TO YOU, OLD AND NEW

Write a letter to your past self, explaining how you learned to do something you thought you could never do.

Be sure to describe what you did, and how you kept going to achieve it. Mention how it felt to finally do it and say who noticed.

THIS ACTIVITY EARNS YOU TWO THING-SPRING POINTS

Write a letter to your future self, explaining what you'd like to do but don't think you can.

Be sure to describe what you'll need to do or change to make it possible. Mention how you will feel when you can KEEP GOING and achieve it, and say who will notice.

THIS ACTIVITY EARNS YOU TWO THING-SPRING POINTS

# BALANCING ACT

You need a healthy balance of support and challenge to help your THING-SPRINGS grow. They need to be as long, strong, and stretchy as each other. If you've had too much support or too much challenge, you'll find it harder to feel balanced and BE RESILIENT!

Fill these THING-SPRINGS with all the good and difficult things you've experienced.

If they're not balanced, try adding some extra support by talking to your SUPPORT TEAM for ideas of THINGS to add, or some extra challenge by thinking of some big, new, scary, or difficult THINGS you could try and add those as well.

SUPPORT

CHALLENGE

GOOD THINGS

DIFFICULT THINGS

Complete this picture and add details to make it a fun, exciting image.

While you're drawing your picture, imagine traveling along the tightrope with your THING-SPRINGS firmly attached to you.

It will be tricky! You'll need excellent balance.

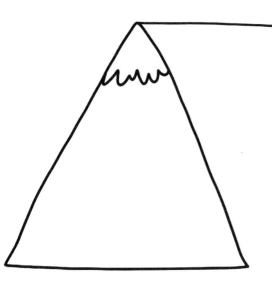
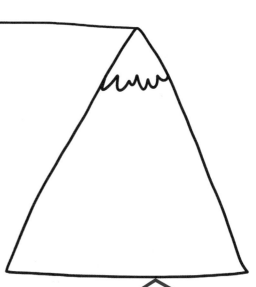

When the picture is finished, make a mind movie where you move along the whole length of the tightrope.

Be sure to feel the THING-SPRINGS wobble underneath you as you carefully KEEP GOING through the tricky sensations.

THIS ACTIVITY EARNS YOU **THREE THING-SPRING** POINTS

# MMM: MARVELOUS MINDFUL MOMENTS

Make a set of MARVELOUS MINDFUL MOMENT cards to cut out and carry with you everywhere you go. That way, you'll always have a solution at your fingertips when you're finding it hard to BE RESILIENT!

Choose your two favorite activities for each HERO in this book that suit the headings on the cards and write out the instructions. Put one activity on each side of the card. If you prefer, you can draw reminders to illustrate the cards.

Cut out the whole page along the dotted line, then cut out each card. Ask someone in your SUPPORT SQUAD for help if you like.

Keep your set of MARVELOUS MINDFUL MOMENT cards safely together and whip them out whenever you need a bounce boost to help you BE RESILIENT!

Look for us HERO characters on the activity pages to match our activities to the cards.

THIS ACTIVITY EARNS YOU TWO THING-SPRING POINTS

# HOPE

## REST & RELAX

HOPE believes that
good things are possible.

# ENERGY

## MOVE

ENERGY puts effort into
making good things happen.

# RESILIENCE

## CREATE

RESILIENCE believes in overcoming
challenges to KEEP GOING.

# OPTIMISM

## IMAGINE

OPTIMISM believes in the power
to succeed.

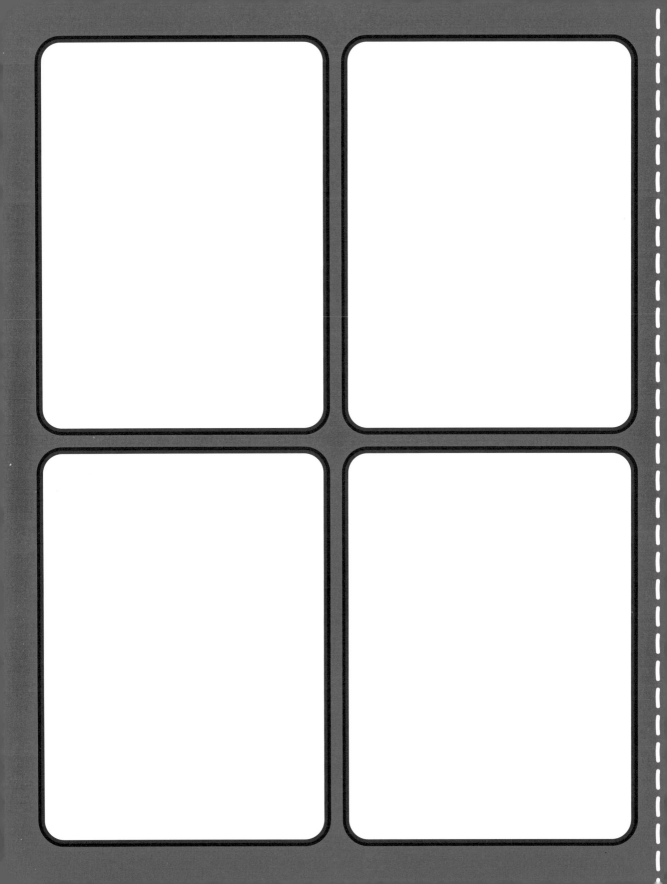

# YOU HERO!

Put yourself in the frame by completing this poster to celebrate your becoming the newest member of your HERO TEAM.

Write your superpower on the podium.

Make sure your costume expresses who you are and design your own logo to represent what you believe.

Don't forget to add your initial to your badge.

Your superpower is what you believe about yourself. Go back and check out the HERO TEAM superpowers if you need help.

INTRODUCING

_ _ _ _ _ _ _ _ _ _ _ _

THIS ACTIVITY EARNS YOU FIVE THING-SPRING POINTS

# HEALTHY THING-SPRINGS

Your THING-SPRINGS are very resilient, but they need a bit of care and attention to keep them in tip-top condition and protect them from all the THINGS that could wear them out. Read how to keep them healthy so you can sit back and BE RESILIENT!

COLOR IN EACH CHECK MARK WHEN YOU'VE READ AND UNDERSTOOD THE INFORMATION ABOUT KEEPING YOUR THING-SPRINGS HEALTHY.

## OIL YOUR THING-SPRINGS

It's VERY important to drink plenty of water. Make sure you have water in the morning, afternoon, and whenever you eat. This keeps your THING-SPRINGS flexible and bouncy.

## MOVE YOUR THING-SPRINGS

Moving is a great way to strengthen and stretch your muscles, and it also improves your balance. All this adds to your confidence and makes your THING-SPRINGS really resilient. Aim to move your body for at least an hour a day, or even more if you like!

Always try to make someone's day with all the THINGS you do and say!

## ✓ FEED YOUR THING-SPRINGS

A balanced diet with lots of fresh fruit and vegetables is the best fuel for your THING-SPRINGS. It's OK to have a few treats here and there, but focus on putting the best fuel in and you'll get the best bounce out. Food has a big impact on your mood and confidence, so help your resilience by eating healthily. Sugary foods and drinks use up your energy quickly and leave your bounce a bit flat.

## ✓ REST YOUR THING-SPRINGS

Rest, relaxation, and recovery time are essential to the well-being of your THING-SPRINGS. Make sure you leave time in your busy day for plenty of each and you'll work better, play better, sleep better, and feel better. This will keep your THING-SPRINGS as strong and stretchy as possible to help you BE RESILIENT! whenever you need to be.

## ✓ COMFORT YOUR THING-SPRINGS

Everything's more fun when you have others to bounce confidently through life with. Take time to build up the THING-SPRINGS of others through your kindness, friendship, and thoughtfulness. You'll benefit from the effort you put in because strong relationships are essential for helping you to BE RESILIENT!

THIS
ACTIVITY EARNS YOU
FOUR THING-SPRING
POINTS

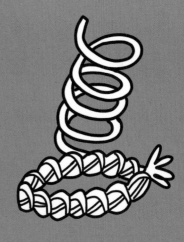

Don't forget to add the name of the person who gave you the compliment.

And remember to let them know how much their kind words mean to you.

Show your SUPPORT SQUAD the compliments if you want – they might have a few more for you!

THIS ACTIVITY EARNS YOU **TWO THING-SPRING** POINTS

# BUBBLE UP

Start by drawing a picture of yourself inside the bubble. Get into a comfortable position, lying down, or sitting if you prefer. Ask a member of your SUPPORT TEAM to read out the instructions for this activity, if you want.

Start your 3:5 breathing from earlier in the book, or you could try Finger Breathing.

## FINGER BREATHING

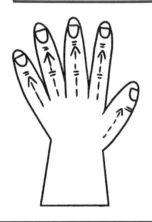

Spread out the fingers on one hand. Slowly and smoothly trace your other pointer finger up your thumb, breathing in as you do.

Stop at the tip, hold your breath for a second, then trace back down the other side as you breathe out.

Trace every finger in the same way. Remember to keep your breathing smooth. Repeat this a few times, and make sure all your attention is on your hand and your breath.

When you notice you're feeling relaxed, imagine yourself rising up, safely and smoothly, on your THING-SPRINGS, high up into the sky, protected by a big bubble all around you. Stretch those coils as far as they go. Focus on feeling completely relaxed, safe, and comfortable. Imagine the landscape below you. See whatever you want to see. Spend five minutes imagining yourself calmly and gently sitting above the landscape, as if you're really there. How does it feel?

Now, imagine all the big, new, scary, or difficult things just bouncing off your beautiful bubble. They can't get through to you or make you wobble. You can feel more and more resilient inside your bubble, to build up your bounce so you can tackle those things in your own time. Picture yourself succeeding at whatever you want to do. Stay as long as you want in your bubble, then bring yourself gently back down to the ground.

# AND SO, TO SLEEP...

Sleep is essential if you're going to BE RESILIENT!

Your brain, muscles, organs, confidence, and mood all rely on you having enough rest and recovery time. While you sleep, wonderful things happen inside you.

You clear away the day's worries, strengthen and stretch your THING-SPRINGS, and prepare for more opportunities to bounce and grow your resilience.

## WHAT DO YOU NEED FOR A GOOD NIGHT'S SLEEP?

Fill these pillowcases with all the things that help you settle down each night.

If there's something you need that you don't have, talk to a member of your SUPPORT SQUAD to see if anything can be done about it.

Fill this blanket with all the good THINGS you'd love to dream about. You can draw, write, or stick on pictures and photos. Come back to this page night after night and keep adding to it.

Talk through the things you've included with someone from your SUPPORT SQUAD if you want.

THIS ACTIVITY EARNS YOU FIVE THING-SPRING POINTS

# AWARDS CEREMONY

Celebrate all your achievements since you started this book.

Write all the THINGS you've achieved on the medals, then award them to yourself in an imaginary ceremony.

If you need to, look back through the book or pop open your I CAN CAN and remind yourself of everything you've achieved.

Pay close attention to how proud the audience members are and how loudly they are cheering for you.

If you prefer, invite your SUPPORT SQUAD along and talk through why you deserve these medals.

You could copy the medals onto cardboard and award them to members of your SUPPORT SQUAD to thank them for the help they've given you along the way. Make sure *you* get these medals though – you've earned them!

# I HAVE CHANGED

COLOR THIS IN

# I WILL CHANGE AGAIN

COLOR THIS IN

**YOU DID IT!**
**BOUNCE FOR JOY!**

Write your name on this certificate or ask a member of your SUPPORT SQUAD to do it. If you want, cut it out and put it somewhere to show everyone what you've achieved.

THIS IS TO CERTIFY THAT

is a
RESILIENCE SUPERSTAR!

Congratulations on your

INCREDIBLE ABILITY TO KEEP GOING!

Signed with great pride,

Your
HERO TEAM:    Hope        ENERGY

Optimism        Resilience

Dr. Sharie    Dr. Sharie

# GO FOR IT!

Now that you have all the skills you need to help you BE RESILIENT! and bounce confidently through life, it's time to start putting them into practice every day.

Write three things you'd like to achieve with your bouncy BE RESILIENT! skills beside the springs. This will help you strengthen and stretch your THING-SPRINGS long after you close this book for the last time.

GO FOR IT - WE ALL
BELIEVE IN YOU!
DR. SHARIE DOES, TOO!

THIS WEEK

THIS YEAR

IN THE FUTURE

## THE BIT FOR GROWN-UPS

## BE RESILIENT! AN ACTIVITY BOOK TO HELP CHILDREN AND YOUNG PEOPLE BOUNCE CONFIDENTLY THROUGH LIFE

This activity book is perfect for parents and caregivers, teachers, learning mentors, social workers, coaches, therapists, and youth leaders who want to help young people develop healthy resilience and confidence.

Being successful is a pressure that children are constantly exposed to in the modern world, and it can feel like popularity and perfection are the most important aspects of success. As children grow, make inevitable mistakes, and learn, they experience many internal and external pressures. These can cause them to doubt themselves, be fearful of failure, compare themselves with others, and feel that they aren't good enough.

In a loving and nurturing environment, children are already becoming resilient and will often work through worries without needing additional help. Despite this, some children become overwhelmed and struggle to make sense of what's going on without the language or tools to explain their distress. Their worries can damage their confidence and reduce their capacity for resilience.

This book enables your child to explore, express, and explain their self-doubts and open up the conversation with you. The fun activities increase their ability to deal with challenges positively, keep going, and try again as they tackle things that are big, new, scary, or difficult, and to bounce back after a setback. Children are encouraged to ask for help, develop positive relationships, and understand the best ways for them to overcome the tricky feelings and challenges they'll face.

When children are experiencing difficulties, you might notice an increase in self-doubt and negative thoughts, along with complaints of stomachaches, headaches, or tiredness, and avoidance of previously enjoyed activities, places, and people. If your child's reluctance or inability to overcome challenges escalates rather than decreases, talk to their school, your doctor, a counselor, or one of the organizations listed below for support and guidance.

### NATIONAL ALLIANCE ON MENTAL ILLNESS (NAMI)

Educate, advocate, listen, lead.

The NAMI HelpLine can be reached Monday through Friday, 10 am–6 pm, ET.

NAMI is the nation's largest grassroots mental health organization dedicated to building better lives for the millions of Americans affected by mental illness.

www.nami.org

Tel: 1-800-950-NAMI (6264)
info@nami.org

### GOODTHERAPY.ORG®

Helping people find therapists.
Advocating for ethical therapy.

GoodTherapy.org offers a directory to help you in your search for a therapist. Using the directory, you can search by therapist location, specialization, gender, and age group treated. If you search by location, your results will include the therapists near you and will display their credentials, location, and the issues they treat.

Tel: 1-888-563-2112 ext. 1
www.goodtherapy.org

### NATIONAL PARENT HELPLINE

Support and resources for parents worried about their children.

Tel: 1-855-4A PARENT
(1-855-427-2736)

nationalparenthelpline.org